I REAL LIFE

Rachel Delahaye

Illustrated by **Roxana de Rond**

OXFORD
UNIVERSITY PRESS

Letter from the Author

I like video games, chatting on social media, and of course I like writing. That means I spend *a lot* of my time looking at screens.

Thankfully, I have a dog called Rocket who begs me to go out at least twice a day. If I ignore him, he jumps up and hits my keyboard with his paws! I'm glad I have such a demanding dog because when I'm with Rocket, I remember how wonderful the outdoors is. The wind, rain and sun on my face make me feel alive, and there's nothing more invigorating than chasing Rocket across a field.

After a dog walk I always feel alert, healthier and more in touch with nature. I wrote this story to remind myself and all of you that the world is our playground. We must step outside and play, before we forget it exists.

Rachel Delahaye

Chapter One

'Bye Dad, see you later!'

Suki slipped on her shoes and swung her bag over her shoulder. She could hear the walking train coming – it was time to go.

Most of the kids who lived in her road went to the same school, and they all walked there together. Suki loved the walking train because she got to chat about homework, TV and video games before school started.

'Wait, Suki!' her dad called. He came out of the kitchen with her little sister in his arms.

'What is it? I've got to go!' Suki could hear the hubbub of voices as the train got closer.

'Mum just texted,' said Dad. 'You know the new family who just moved in opposite us? They have a boy who's starting at your school today. Mum said you'd walk to school with him.'

'But I promised Katya I'd walk with her,' groaned Suki. 'We have to talk about Ninja Girls stuff. It's important.'

Ninja Girls was a video game, and it was all Suki thought about, day and night.

'You can chat to Katya at break time, Suki,' said Dad. He popped Lucy in her buggy. 'I'll come over the road with you.'

Suki felt like stamping her feet.

'But Katya is waiting for me. Why didn't Mum tell me before?' she said.

'She had an early shift at work. Go on – run and tell Katya, and then we'll go and find the new boy.'

A few minutes later, Suki was outside the new neighbours' house. Her skin was prickling with annoyance. She knew she had to smile, but her face felt as heavy as stone. The door was opened by a woman holding a baby. Dad stepped forward.

'Mrs Gray? Hello, I'm Dan and this is my daughter, Suki. That's Lucy in the buggy.'

'Ah, the neighbours!' said Mrs Gray. She turned to Suki. 'Tom's been so excited about meeting you and having someone his own age to play with. Tom! Time to go!'

Footsteps thundered down stairs, and a boy with shaggy hair appeared at his mother's side.

'Let's go!' he grinned.

'I told you he was excited,' Mrs Gray laughed. 'Something tells me you two are going to be good friends.'

'I'm sure they will, and Suki will be delighted to show Tom around,' said Suki's dad.

Suki gave a small smile, but inside her stomach was knotted. All she wanted to do was hang out with Katya, and now she had to look after a strange-looking boy who had no friends. He'd probably never even heard of the Ninja Girls.

Chapter Two

'I've never heard of them,' Tom said. 'Are they a pop group?'

'No,' sighed Suki. 'Ninja Girls is a video game. I play it every afternoon with my best friend. We're obsessed. I reckon I'll get my black belt in Ninja Tricks soon.'

'What does that mean?'

'Ninja Tricks give you special powers for fighting monsters,' she explained.

'What monsters?' asked Tom.

'Shadow Monsters,' said Suki. 'They're the Ninja Girls' worst enemy.'

'Why do the Ninja Girls have enemies?'

'Never mind …' Suki sighed.

She had been right. Tom didn't know anything about Ninja Girls. In fact, he didn't even seem to understand how video games worked! Thank goodness they'd arrived at school so she didn't have to talk to him anymore.

'Here we are,' said Suki, at the gates of Fillbridge Primary School. 'What class are you in?'

Tom looked at his hand, where he'd scrawled something in pen. 'Class 4B.'

'Great,' Suki said, feeling a little deflated. 'Same as me. Come on – it's this way.'

Suki showed Tom where to hang his coat and bag, and then took him into the classroom. The rest of her friends were already there, and they stared as she appeared with the new boy.

'Where have you been?' said Allison.

'You missed the train. Were you waiting on the wrong platform?' laughed James. It was a joke the teachers always made if they were late for school.

'Who's your friend?' shouted Pablo.

'This is Tom,' Suki said, blushing. 'He's new.'

13

Suki didn't know what to do or say after that, so she quickly sat down next to Katya and left Tom standing by the door.

'I hope I don't have to walk with him every day. He's so boring,' Suki whispered.

'What if your mum's arranged for you to play with him after school?' Katya said.

'I hope not. I'd rather die!' Suki said, dramatically.

There was a hush as Mrs Prest bustled in. Her arms were piled so high with exercise books she couldn't see a thing, and she bumped right into Tom. With a yelp, she dropped her books and the class laughed.

'He must be so embarrassed,' Katya giggled.

But Tom didn't seem embarrassed at all. He helped Mrs Prest pick the books up and then introduced himself.

'Hi, I'm Tom Gray. I'm new.'

'Welcome, Tom,' said Mrs Prest. 'Now, where shall I put you … ?'

Mrs Prest looked around the class, and the children shuffled closer to their friends.

'Katya, why don't you move next to Lily, and then Tom can sit next to Suki. Why don't you two introduce yourselves?'

'We've already met,' Tom said. 'We're neighbours.'

17

'Excellent!' Mrs Prest said. 'In that case, Suki, you can be Tom's buddy until he finds his feet.'

Suki was no longer able to manage even the tiniest of smiles.

Tom sat down next to her. 'Don't worry,' he whispered. 'You don't have to be my buddy. I can look after myself.'

'No, it's fine,' Suki sighed.

'I don't mind being on my own. I like it sometimes. It gives me a chance to watch people.' Tom smiled and opened his pencil case. Inside were some fruity sweets. He turned his pencil case so Suki could see.

'Do you want one for break time?'

Suki pulled out a strawberry chew. 'Thanks,' she whispered, and curiosity bubbled inside her. 'Why do you watch people?'

'To see who will play.'

'Play what?' Suki asked. But Mrs Prest clapped her hands for attention and Suki never found out the answer.

For a new kid, Tom Gray was oddly confident. He put his hand up all the time in class and didn't seem to mind if he got a question wrong. And just like he said, he spent break time alone, walking round the playground or disappearing into the wooded areas around it.

Suki and Katya watched Tom from one of the picnic tables as they doodled Ninja Girls characters on their notepads.

'I hope he doesn't think he's our friend now just because you two sit together,' Katya said. 'He's really strange.'

Chapter Three

The next day, Tom joined the train and walked alone at the back. He didn't seem sad about it, though. He spent his breaks alone, too. Sometimes he disappeared into the woods and came back with scuffed shoes and muddy trousers.

'What do you think he does in there?' Katya asked Suki one morning. 'Is he some kind of troll?' The others at the picnic table laughed.

'Why don't you ask him?' said Pablo.

'Because I don't speak troll language,' said Katya, and they laughed some more.

'I tried to talk to him about MineMaker, but he doesn't have a games console. He said he doesn't even have a computer,' Allison confided.

'What does he do, then?' said James.

The others at the bench shook their heads and gathered their snack boxes and went back to class, but Suki pretended she'd lost her pen. The truth was, she wanted to be on her own for a minute. She definitely didn't want to be friends with Tom, but the way the others talked about him was mean. And if he didn't have a games console or a computer, maybe it meant his family didn't have much money. She decided to find out.

The next morning at registration, Tom opened up his pencil case and silently pushed it across to Suki, as he did every day. It was the only time they spoke.

She plucked out a sweet with a red wrapper. 'Tom, can I ask you something?'

'Of course.'

'Are you poor?'

'No, I don't think so. Why?'

'Because Allison said you don't have a games console or a computer. Is that because you can't afford one?' asked Suki.

'No, it's because I don't want one,' Tom replied.

Tom laughed at Suki's shocked expression, and Suki popped the sweet in her mouth so she wouldn't have to say anything else.

Later, at lunch break, they were all chatting about which game was better – Ninja Girls or Skate Park 3.

Suddenly Suki saw Tom heading up the field. He stopped and talked to some of the footballing kids. He even laughed a bit with Jed, who was the noisiest boy in 4B and always played the roughest games.

'What do you think they're talking about?' Katya asked Suki.

'I don't know.'

After a couple of minutes, Jed pointed to the football pitch and Tom shook his head and walked off, back to his hiding place in the woods.

'Maybe he's trying to make friends,' Suki said, realizing that she felt a bit sad.

Perhaps I need to help him, she thought.

After school, Suki made sure she left the classroom at the same time as Tom so she could walk with him to the school gates.

'Hey Tom,' she smiled. 'Do you want to come over and play later?'

Chapter Four

Tom stood at Suki's door wearing jeans, wellies, an anorak and a backpack.

Suki was confused. 'Why have you brought a backpack?'

'Because we need provisions,' said Tom.

'What are provisions?' Suki asked.

'Food, basically.'

'We've got food in the kitchen, silly,' grinned Suki. 'You don't need to bring your own. Do you want to take off your boots and come in? I've loaded up Ninja Girls but if you don't like that, I've got other games. You'll be an expert by teatime!'

Tom didn't make any move to come inside. 'I think I got confused,' he said. 'When you asked if I wanted to come over, I thought I was going to be playing a real-life game with you – not just on the computer.'

'Oh, well, it's the same thing, isn't it?'

'Not really. Put your boots on. Mum's taking my baby brother to the park and we're going, too.'

Tom started to walk away and Suki didn't know what to do. With a frustrated grunt, she pulled her wellies on, and called down the hallway to her mum.

'I'm going to the park with Tom!'

Mum appeared with Lucy wriggling in her arms. 'That's great! Glad you two are getting on. Have a good time.'

Suki huffed to herself and ran to catch up with Tom.

When they got to the park, Mrs Gray was already settling the baby into the bucket swing. Tom looked as excited as if they were at a fairground. Suki looked around at the muddy grass, the thicket of trees and the old climbing frame. She hadn't been to this park in ages, and she remembered why – it was rubbish.

'This place is great!' Tom shouted. 'Ready to play?'

Suki stood in the middle of the park with her arms by her sides. Urgh! Katya was right. Tom Gray was strange, and now she was stuck 'playing' with him.

'Here,' he said, handing her a long stick. 'You'll need this to defend yourself.' He had one, too. 'It's a good thing you've had ninja training,' he continued. 'You're going to need that where we're going.'

'Where are we going?' asked Suki.

'In there,' he said, pointing to the wooded area. 'We need to make our way round the edge and through the middle and end up at the gate. That's when we know we're safe.'

'Safe from what?'

'Shadow Monsters.'

'Oh, Shadow Monsters, right,' said Suki. 'You're copying Ninja Girls.'

'Don't be silly, said Tom. 'Ninja Girls copied the real thing! The real Shadow Monsters lurk behind trees. Their goal is to stop good people getting to the Safe Zone.'

'And we're good people?'

'Yes,' said Tom seriously. 'You're a very good person, which means they will be desperate to stop you.'

'I'd like to see them try!' Suki giggled.

'Come on, then,' Tom grinned and spun his stick in the air. Then he caught it and gripped it tightly. 'Let's go!'

'Let's go!' Suki repeated, not understanding where her sudden burst of enjoyment had come from.

Tom and Suki ran towards the trees and as soon as they set foot in the empty woodland, long shadows fell on them.

'Suki, to your left! Attack!' Tom suddenly yelled.

39

Suki swung her stick, cracking it across the closest shadow three times. 'Tom, look out!' she shouted, cheering as Tom did a ninja spin, kicking out at the Shadow Monster with his right leg and knocking it to the floor.

He stood, panting. 'The woods are full of them,' he said. 'We need to look out for each other. Come on, this way.'

Chapter Five

Tom and Suki tiptoed through the woods, eyes peeled for Shadow Monsters, hiding behind trees whenever there was a rustle. It might just have been birds, but they couldn't take any chances. When they came across a good climbing tree, Tom held up his hand.

'Stop. This is the perfect place to refuel. Follow me.'

They climbed onto a branch, facing each other. Tom opened his backpack and brought out two chocolate bars.

'We've earned this,' Suki said, eyes twinkling.

'We certainly have,' nodded Tom. 'But the journey isn't over yet. We need to go over the Bridge of Doom and then run across the Gloomy Plains to the Safe Zone. Are you ready?'

'I'm ready.'

Running as fast as they could, they leaped onto the rusty climbing frame – the Bridge of Doom – and crossed the bars, with Shadow Monsters snapping at their feet.

Finally, they dashed across the Gloomy Plains to the park gate, and collapsed in an exhausted heap. Suki was wet and muddy but for some reason she couldn't stop laughing.

'Is this what you do in the woods at school?' Suki asked as they walked home.

'Sometimes,' said Tom. 'Sometimes I just sit and think. It depends on my mood.'

Suki laughed, 'Maybe you'd make more friends at school if you acted normal. Like Jed.'

'Jed? We're already friends. He fought a lot of Shadow Monsters after school yesterday. That's what we were talking about at lunch.'

Suki looked stunned.

'I told you, I watch people and see who wants to play,' Tom said. 'Most people want to. But some people let their computers do all the playing and forget how to play in real life. They just need a bit of help to remember.'

Suki smiled. 'I'd forgotten how much fun it is to run and jump and go wild! Now I can do both – play computer games when I'm on my own, and outside games when I'm not!'

'I'm coming to the park again tomorrow, if you're interested ... ' Tom said.

Suki paused, looking serious.

'I don't think you should go to the park on your own. Not with all those Shadow Monsters around. You need someone who can protect you.'

'Like who?'

Suki pointed to herself and grinned.

'A real life Ninja Girl, of course! See you tomorrow. You bring the sticks and I'll bring the provisions!'